SOLVING SCIENCE MYSTERIES

Why Does My Heart Pump?

All About the Human Body

Helen Bethune

PowerKiDS press™

New York

Published in 2010 by The Rosen Publishing Group, Inc.
29 East 21st Street, New York, NY 10010

Produced and designed by Denise Ryan & Associates
Editors: Helen Moore and Edwina Hamilton
Designer: Anita Adams
Photographer: Lyz Turner-Clark
U.S. Editor: Kara Murray

Photo Credits: pp. 4 and 5 left © Photographer: Sebastian Kaulitzki | Agency: Dreamstime.com; pp. 5 right, 9 right, 13 top, 13 bottom, 14 top DK Images; pp. 6 and 7 top © Photographer: Dannyphoto80 | Agency: Dreamstime.com; p. 8 Fotolibra; p. 11 top right: David Lewis; p. 15 top © Photographer: Andrey Kiselev | Agency: Dreamstime.com; p. 15 bottom left: Mary Gascho; p. 15 bottom right: Susan Stevenson; p. 16: National Research Canada; p. 17: Photolibrary; p. 18: Richard Cisar-Wright © Newspix; p. 18 bottom: © Deb Schwedhelm Photography.

Library of Congress Cataloging-in-Publication Data

Bethune, Helen.
  Why does my heart pump? all about the human body / Helen Bethune.
      p. cm. — (Solving science mysteries)
  Includes index.
  ISBN 978-1-4488-0403-0 (library binding) — ISBN 978-1-4488-0404-7 (pbk.) —
ISBN 978-1-4488-0405-4 (6-pack)
  1. Human physiology—Juvenile literature. I. Title.
  QP37.B48 2010
  612—dc22

                                    2009038260

Manufactured in the United States of America

CPSIA Compliance Information: Batch #WW10PK: For Further Information contact Rosen Publishing, New York, New York at 1-800-237-9932

Contents

Questions About Bones

Q: How do our bones move?

A: Different types of joints allow our bones to move in different ways. Elbows, fingers, knees, and toes all have hinged joints. They allow our arms, hands, legs, and toes to bend and straighten. Ball-and-socket joints in our shoulders and hips allow movement in many directions. The sliding joints in our spines allow us to bend and stretch.

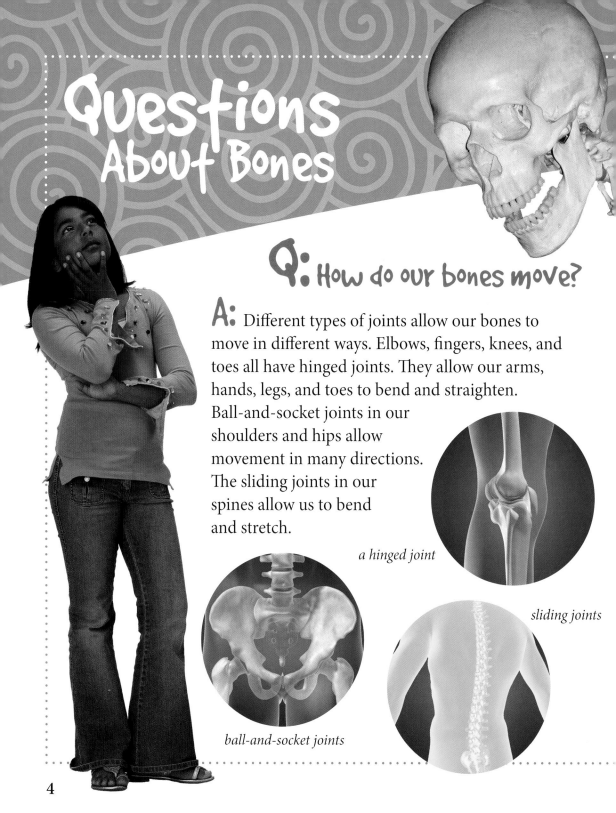

a hinged joint

sliding joints

ball-and-socket joints

Q: Why don't bones rub against each other and what holds them together?

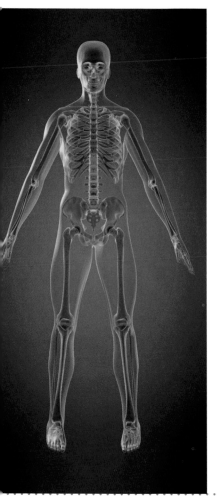

A: Cartilage prevents our bones from rubbing against each other at the joints. Cartilage is a soft, flexible substance that supports and protects the bones. Although cartilage is soft, it also stands up to a lot of wear, allowing bones to slide smoothly past one another. It is a little like a pillow and cushions the ends of the joints.

Strong, fibrous straps of tissue called ligaments, which are like strong rubber bands, hold the bones together. Joints have their own special fluid to help them move freely.

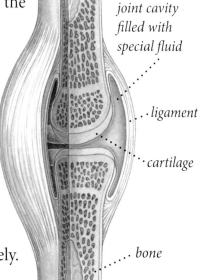

joint cavity filled with special fluid

ligament

cartilage

bone

Questions About the Heart and Blood

Q: What is the difference between arteries and veins?

A: Arteries and veins are the vessels that carry blood around the body. Arteries carry blood from the heart. They have thick walls to withstand the blood being pumped from the heart. Thinner-walled veins carry blood back to the heart. Blood is the body's transport system. It provides the oxygen and nutrients our bodies need. It also carries away waste. When blood is no longer carrying oxygen, it is carrying waste to be processed by other organs in the body. The heart, blood, and blood vessels make up the body's circulatory system.

Arteries and veins divide into even smaller vessels, called capillaries. The capillaries distribute blood throughout the body.

Q: Why does my heart pump?

A: The heart, which is a muscle, pumps because it has to move blood around your body. It is a **dual** pump. The left side sends blood to the body, providing it with oxygen and nutrients. The right side sends blood back to the lungs, carrying waste it has picked up.

The heart is divided into four chambers. The top chambers, the atria, hold the incoming blood. The two bottom chambers, the ventricles, pump blood out of the heart. The atria and the ventricles **contract** as they pump, making the sound of the heartbeat.

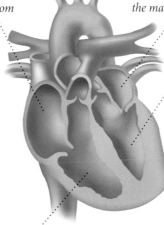

The left atrium receives fresh blood from the lungs.

The right atrium receives blood from the main veins.

The right ventricle receives blood from the right atrium and pumps it to the lungs.

The left ventricle receives blood from the left atrium and pumps it to the body.

A system of valves makes sure that the blood follows a one-way route through the heart to the lungs and back.

Feel That Beat!

Because your heart has to pump so much blood through your body, you can feel a little thump in your arteries each time your heart beats. The thump is called the pulse. Try putting two fingers on the inside of your wrist and you may be able to feel your heartbeat.

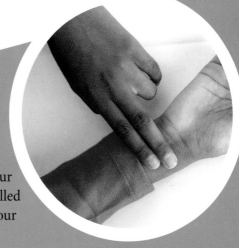

Questions About our Insides

Q: Why does blood need cleaning?

A: Your blood needs cleaning because if your kidneys did not filter it, chemical wastes would build up in your body and become **toxic**. As your body uses nutrients, it produces waste. The blood carries any waste or leftovers—for example, you might already have enough of a particular **vitamin** in your body—to your kidneys to filter. Your kidneys are two bean-shaped organs at the back of your **abdomen**. They remove chemical wastes and excess water as often as 400 times a day. Wastes drain out of your body as urine. There are more than one million tiny filters inside the kidneys all working hard to keep you healthy!

renal artery

renal vein

ureter

To find your kidneys, put your hands on your hips, then slide your hands up until you can feel your ribs. Put your thumbs on your back and you will know where your kidneys are.

Q: What does the liver do?

A: The liver carries out many tasks. It filters blood from the intestines and strains out harmful substances or wastes, turning some of the waste into **bile**. The liver figures out how many nutrients will go to the rest of the body and how many will stay behind in storage. For example, the liver stores certain vitamins and a type of sugar your body uses for energy. It also removes debris, destroys poisons, worn-out cells and alcohol, and **manufactures** vitamin A and many other chemicals the body needs.

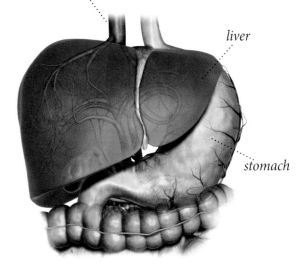

hepatic vein

liver

stomach

Questions About the Face

Q: Does my face use muscles?

A: Yes, it does. Unlike other muscles, facial muscles are not attached directly to bones. Many of them are attached to the skin. If you contract your facial muscles even a little, you can make many different expressions. Why not watch your facial muscles at work?

Q: Is the tongue a muscle?

A: Yes, the tongue is a muscle that is attached only at one end. It contains 18 interwoven muscles that make it very flexible. This is necessary for us to be able to speak, chew, and swallow.

The tongue is also responsible for our sense of taste, which comes from cells called taste buds. Most taste buds are on the surface of the tongue but they are also in the roof of the mouth and in the throat.

Q: Why do we sneeze?

A: We sneeze when something gets trapped in the **mucus** inside our noses. The inside of the nose is lined with a moist, thin layer of tissue called a mucous membrane. The mucous membrane makes mucus. Mucus captures dust, germs, and other small particles that could irritate your lungs. There are also hairs inside your nose that can trap large particles, such as dirt or **pollen**. If something does get trapped in the mucus, it makes you sneeze. Sneezes can send foreign particles speeding out of your nose at 99 miles per hour (160 km/h)!

It's a Fact

> What a Giggle!

Scientists say that being ticklish is our defense against insects such as spiders and bugs. That is why **vulnerable** parts of our bodies—our feet, chest, and armpits—tend to be the most ticklish.

> Bone Up!

At birth, your body had about 300 bones. By the time you are an adult, these bones will have fused to form 206 bones.

> Beware: Yawning Is Contagious!

Have you ever noticed that if you yawn, the people around you do, too? Scientists cannot agree on exactly why we yawn but they all agree that it is contagious!

> All Ears

The smallest bone in the human body is located in the ear. The stapes, or stirrup bone, is the only bone that is fully grown at birth.

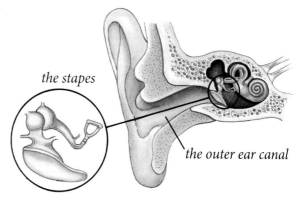

the stapes

the outer ear canal

> Earwax

Earwax traps dirt and stops it from getting into your ear. It is made in the outer ear canal. It either falls out or comes out when you wash your hair.

the ulnar nerve

It's Not Funny!

Your funny bone is not a bone at all. It is the ulnar nerve, which runs down the inside part of your elbow. If this nerve is bumped against the humerus, the long bone that starts at your elbow and goes up to your shoulder, it gives you a tingling feeling.

the humerus

the elbow

Can You Believe It?

the rib cage

the diaphragm

It's a Gas!

When you swallow food, you also swallow air. Some of this air travels through your digestive system with your food. The air has to escape your body somehow, and it comes out as flatus. You probably call it something else!

Hic!

Charles Osborne (1894–1991) started to hiccup when he was 28 years old. His hiccups began after he tried to lift a pig, probably straining his diaphragm muscle, the source of hiccups. He hiccuped for 69 years! At first he hiccuped 40 times a minute, then 20 times a minute. He stopped hiccuping one year before his death.

Laughing lowers levels of stress and strengthens the immune system. Six year olds laugh an average of 300 times a day. Adults laugh only 15 to 100 times a day.

ADCHOO!

"ADCHOO" does not just sound like a sneeze. It also stands for "Autosomal Dominant Compelling Helio-Opthalmic Outburst syndrome." This is the scientific name given to a condition in which, when someone is exposed to a bright light, he or she sneezes. These people are also called photic sneezers.

Surface Area

The skin is the largest human organ, with a surface area of about 25 square feet (2.3 sq m). That's about the same size as a large tablecloth.

A snore can be almost as loud as the noise of a pneumatic drill.

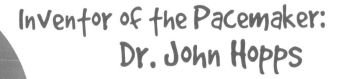

Who Found Out?

Inventor of the Pacemaker: Dr. John Hopps

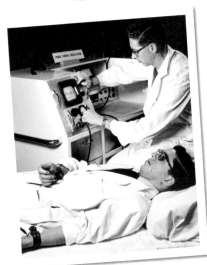

Canadian John Hopps (1919–1998) invented the first heart pacemaker, a device that makes the heart continue to beat. In 1941, he was researching **hypothermia** at the National Research Council. He was trying to restore body temperature with radio frequency heating. He found that if a heart stopped beating due to cooling, it could be restarted by **stimulation**. This led to his invention of the heart pacemaker.

The first pacemakers had to be used outside the body, as they were too big to be placed inside it. Today's pacemakers are small and can be inserted into the body. In 1984 Dr. Hopps himself had to have one fitted.

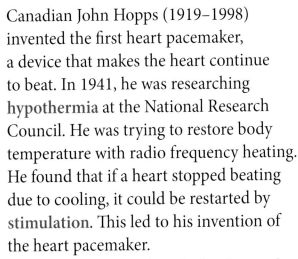

Pioneer in open-Heart Surgery: Dr. Daniel Hale Williams

The first open-heart **surgery** was performed by the African-American physician Dr. Daniel Hale Williams (1856–1931) in 1893. He founded and worked at the Provident Hospital and Training School, in Chicago, the first hospital to be run by African Americans in America. It became famous for its advanced **sterilization** and **antiseptic** methods.

In 1893 a young African-American man named James Cornish was admitted to the hospital. He had been stabbed in the chest. Williams realized that the only way to save the man's life was to open his chest and operate. The operation was a success, mainly because of Dr. Williams's sterilization methods. James Cornish lived another 50 years.

Bionic Ear:
Professor Graeme Clark

Australian surgeon Graeme Milbourne Clark (1935–) pioneered the multiple-channel cochlear implant (bionic ear), which has brought hearing and speech understanding to tens of thousands of people with severe to profound hearing loss in countries all over the world. Professor Clark's original research started in 1967 and the first implant in an adult was made in 1978. The bionic ear is still being refined and improved today. In 2004 Professor Clark was awarded Australia's highest civil honor, the Companion of the Order of Australia (AC), for his services to medicine and science.

You can see this girl's cochlear implant here, which she received at six years of age.

First Human Heart Transplant Surgeon: Dr. Christiaan Barnard

South-African-born Dr. Christiaan Barnard (1922–2001) performed the first human heart transplant in 1967. This operation involves transferring the heart of a recently deceased person into someone else's body. He had experimented with animal heart transplants and had carried out successful human kidney transplants for several years before he undertook the human heart transplant.

The patient survived with his new heart for 18 days. Dr. Barnard's next heart transplant patient lived for another 19 months. In 1969 he transplanted a new heart into Dorothy Fisher. She lived for 24 years, becoming his longest-surviving heart transplant patient.

It's Quiz Time!

The pages where you can find the answers are shown in the red circles, except where otherwise noted.

Complete this crossword.

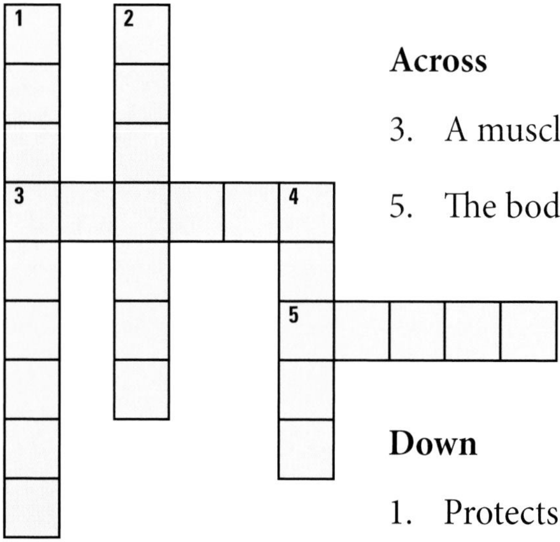

Across

3. A muscle attached at only one end ⑩

5. The body's transport system ⑥

Down

1. Protects bones ⑤

2. Bean-shaped organs ⑧

4. An example of a hinged joint ④

Choose the correct words.

1. Elbows, fingers, knees, and toes all have _ _ _ _ _ _ joints. ④

2. The _ _ _ _ _, _ _ _ _ _, and _ _ _ _ _ _ _ _ _ _ _ make up the circulatory system. ⑥

3. _ _ _ _ _ _ _ _ _ is a soft, flexible substance that supports and protects the bones. ⑤

4. The inside of the nose is lined with a moist, thin layer of _ _ _ _ _ _ called a mucous _ _ _ _ _ _ _ _. ⑪

5. Professor Graeme _ _ _ _ _ invented the _ _ _ _ _ _ ear. ⑱

Try It out!

The first tool used to listen to a person's heartbeat, called a stethoscope, was just a simple wooden tube about 10 inches (25 cm) long. You can make your own simple stethoscope using a paper towel tube! Try listening to how fast each person in your family's heart beats using your cardboard stethoscope.

Write down each family member's name on a piece of paper. Put your tube over the first person's heart and put your ear to the other end. Count the beats for 1 minute (or for 15 seconds and multiply the number you get by four). Write the number of beats next to that person's name. Do this with everyone in your family. Did everyone's heart beat at the same rate?

Now Try This!

Have each person do some jumping jacks for 1 or 2 minutes. Count their heartbeats again. What happened?

Glossary

abdomen (AB-duh-mun) The part of the body that contains the stomach.

antiseptic (an-tee-SEP-tik) Preventing the spread of disease-causing germs.

bile (BY-el) A digestive juice.

contract (kun-TRAKT) To become smaller.

dual (DOO-ul) Double.

hypothermia (hy-puh-THUR-mee-uh) The condition of having a body temperature well below normal.

manufactures (man-yuh-FAK-cherz) Makes something.

mucus (MYOO-kus) A slimy substance.

nutrients (NOO-tree-unts) Nourishing things, particularly for the body and plants.

oxygen (OK-sih-jen) One of the gases in the air that people need to stay alive.

photic (FOH-tik) Having to do with light.

pollen (PAH-lin) A powder made by the male parts of flowers.

sterilization (ster-uh-luh-ZAY-shun) Made free from germs.

stimulation (stim-yuh-LAY-shun) Causing something to happen.

surgery (SER-juh-ree) An operation.

toxic (TOK-sik) Poisonous.

vitamin (VY-tuh-min) A nutrient to help the body fight illness and grow strong.

vulnerable (VUL-neh-reh-bul) Able to harmed or attacked easily.

withstand (with-STAND) To resist or put up with.

Index

Web Sites

Due to the changing nature of Internet links, PowerKids Press has developed an online list of Web sites related to the subject of this book. This site is updated regularly. Please use this link to access the list:

www.powerkidslinks.com/ssm/pump/